HARCOURT ART EVERYWHERE

AUTHORS

Jacqueline Chanda

Kristen Pederson Marstaller

CONSULTANTS

Katherina Danko-McGhee

María Teresa García-Pedroche

Harcourt

SCHOOL PUBLISHERS

Orlando   Austin   New York   San Diego   Toronto   London

Visit *The Learning Site!*

www.harcourtschool.com

ISBN 0-15-336447-5

4 5 6 7 8 9 10   048   13 12 11 10 09 08 07 06

Dear Young Artist,

Did you know that art is all around you? It is in your home and school. It is on TV. Art is created by people and found in nature.

Whenever you notice a beautiful color or an interesting shape, you are thinking like an artist. In this book, you will see art made by all kinds of artists—grown-ups and children your age. You will create your own art. Come on! Let's get started!

Sincerely,
The Authors

3

CONTENTS

Unit 1 — Celebrate Our World 22
Line and Shape

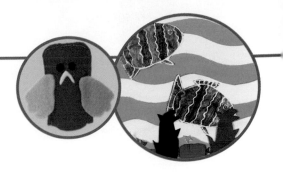

Unit 4

Surprises Everywhere 82
Form and Space

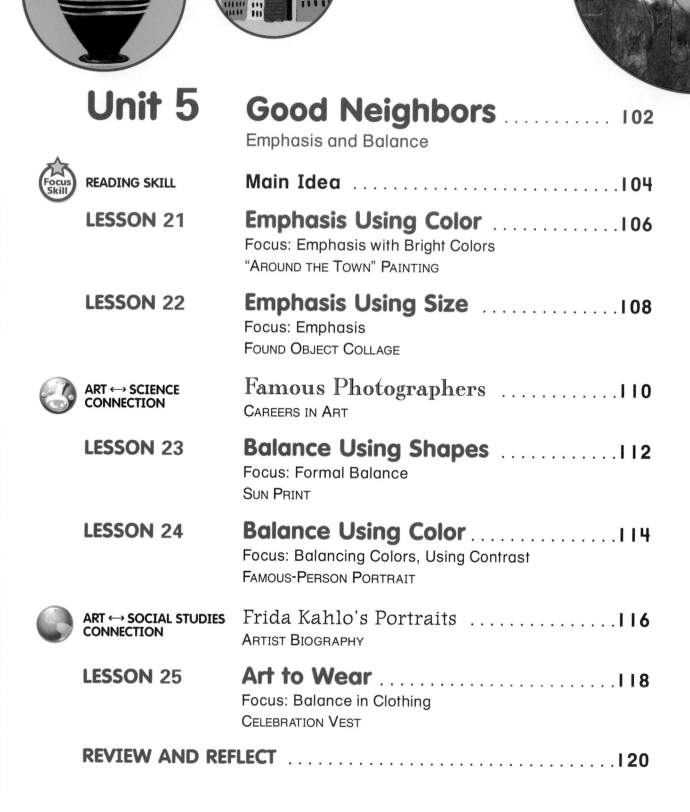

A T   A   G L A N C E

Art Production

Elements and Principles

Media

Cross-Curricular Connections

Artists have many creative ideas. Often, they sketch their ideas.

▲ *Dinosaur Bob* by William Joyce   LITERATURE LINK

The artist William Joyce used the ideas in his sketchbook to make a book.

Keep an art sketchbook. Draw what you see. Sketch your ideas, and write about them.

This leaf is my favorite fall color.

Keep other things like pictures, notes, and colors in your sketchbook.

spiral shell

pyramid

spiral

Visiting a
Museum

▲ Guggenheim Museum, New York City, New York

Walk slowly. Look at the art.

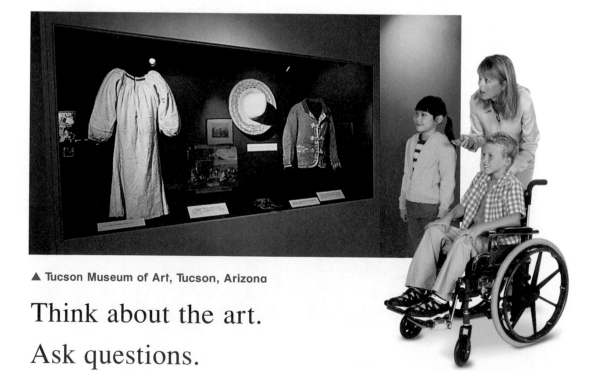

▲ Tucson Museum of Art, Tucson, Arizona

Think about the art.

Ask questions.

▲ Whitney Museum of American Art, New York City, New York

Talk quietly. Tell what you think about the art. Find out what others think.

▲ Dallas Museum of Art, Dallas, Texas

Sketch what you see. Draw or write ideas the art makes you think of.

A title tells what a lesson is about.

Lesson
10

Vocabulary

seascape
horizon
line

Colors in Seascapes

What is going on in this painting? A **seascape** is an artwork that shows a water setting, like the sea. What colors did the artist use to show water? Why?

A caption tells the name of the artist and artwork.

Winslow Homer, *Gloucester Harbor*

Highlighted words help you learn art vocabulary.

Can you find the line where the sky and the water meet? This is called the **horizon line**.

58

16

Look for other important parts of your book.

- Title Page
- Contents
- Glossary

Artist's Workshop

Crayon-Resist Seascape

PLAN

Think about all the things you can find on the ocean and in the ocean.

CREATE

1. Draw a horizon line. Use crayons to draw boats. Add plants and animals under the water.

2. Paint watercolor over the picture. Make it darker at the bottom.

The <u>steps</u> are in order. They tell how to make an artwork.

REFLECT

What colors did you use? What does the water look like?

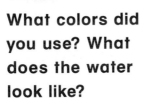

Where can you find a seascape in your town?

59

Elements of Art

Art is made up of parts called **elements**. Here are elements you will learn about.

line ▼

color ▲

shape ▼

SCHOOL

See also Elements and
Principles, pages 170–181.

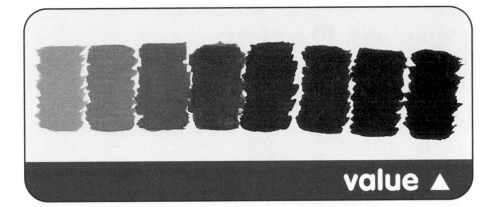

value ▲

space ▲

texture ▼

form ▼

OLD FASHIONED
OATS
100% Natural

NET WT. 18 OZ (1 LB 2 OZ) 510g

19

Principles of Design

Artists use art elements in different ways according to **principles**. Here are principles you will learn about.

balance ▲

emphasis ▼

pattern ▲

See also Elements and Principles, pages 170–181.

movement ▼

rhythm ▼

unity ▲

variety ▲

▲ Grandma Moses, *Autumn*

LOCATE IT

This painting is in the Bennington Museum in Bennington, Vermont.

See Maps of Museums and Art Sites, pages 144–147.

Bennington, VT

Celebrate Our World

I'm Glad

I'm glad the sky is
painted blue,
And the earth is
painted green,
With such a lot of
nice fresh air
All sandwiched
in between.

Anonymous

Unit Vocabulary

lines

outline

movement

geometric
shapes

free-form
shapes

organic shapes

portrait

self-portrait

ABOUT THE ARTIST

See Gallery of Artists,
pages 182–191.

 Multimedia Art Glossary
Visit *The Learning Site*
www.harcourtschool.com

Make Inferences

What is happening in the picture?

Brian Pinkney,
illustration from *Max Found Two Sticks* LITERATURE LINK

Why does the boy want the sticks? Use
what you see and what you already know to
decide.

Read the paragraph. Make a chart like the one below. Tell what you think.

A man in a uniform throws sticks to the boy. The man has drums, and the sticks are drumsticks. I think the boy will use them to play music.

What I See and Read	+ What I Know =	What I Think
The man has drums. He throws sticks to the boy.	The sticks are drumsticks.	The boy can play music with them.
The man wears a uniform.	People in a band wear uniforms.	The man is in a ____.
The man still holds two drumsticks.	Drummers use two sticks to play the drums.	The man ____.

On Your Own

Look at the painting on pages 22–23. Make a chart. Write what you see and know. Then write what you think.

Lines All Around

What do you see in these artworks?

Pablo Picasso,
Hand with Flowers A

Artists use many kinds of **lines**. Find lines like these in the art.

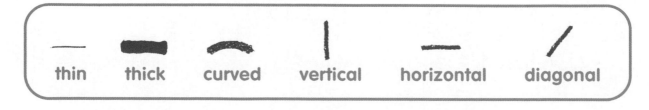

thin   thick   curved   vertical   horizontal   diagonal

An **outline** is the line along the edge of a shape.
Use your finger. Trace an outline in each picture.

Henri Rousseau,
The Banks of the
Bièvre Near Bicêtre

Artist's Workshop

My Fall Tree

1. Draw the outline of a tree.
   Use many kinds of lines.

2. Glue on paper leaves.

Lines Show Movement

What is going on in each artwork?
What actions do you see in each one?

 Diego Rivera,
La Piñata

Lines that curve and bend through an
artwork can show **movement**. Which
lines show movement in these artworks?

Abastenia St. Leger Eberle, **B**
Untitled

28

"Dance for Joy" Drawing

 PLAN

Think about how your arms and legs bend when you are dancing.

CREATE

1. **Draw yourself dancing. Show your arms and legs moving.**

2. **Use lines to show things around you moving.**

REFLECT

Did you bend, jump, or twirl? What kinds of lines did you use to show movement?

What actions do you see in your classroom?

Art in Our World

Lines, shapes, and colors are all around us. You can find them in living things and nonliving things. What lines, shapes, and colors do you see in the pictures?

A Wrought-iron fence

B Texas bluebonnets

C Autumn leaf

The lines on a zebra help keep it safe. These stripes blend in with the lines of tall grass to hide the zebra.

D Zebras

Think About Art

What lines, shapes, and colors do you see in your classroom?

E Railroad crossing sign

Roller coaster **F**

Geometric Shapes

What does this art show? What shapes can you find? Shapes like circles, squares, and triangles are **geometric shapes**.

 Wayne Thiebaud, *Desserts*

circle   oval   triangle   square   rectangle

Trace some geometric shapes in the art. What kinds of lines did the artists use to make the shapes?

Artist's Workshop

Food Collage

1. Cut out geometric shapes to show a meal you like.

2. Glue everything to a paper place mat.

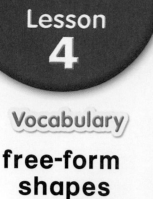

Free-Form Shapes

What do you think this picture is about? Artists use many shapes that are not geometric, called **free-form shapes**.

Henri Matisse, *The Horse, the Rider, and the Clown*

Free-form shapes of things from nature, like animals and plants, are **organic shapes**.

Free-Form Shapes

organic shapes

Free-Form Flip Art

 PLAN

Think about free-form shapes around you.

 CREATE

1. Cut out free-form shapes along the edge of a half sheet of paper.

2. Glue the half sheet to a whole sheet. Glue the free-form shapes.

 REFLECT

What free-form shapes did you make? Are any of them organic shapes?

What organic shapes do you see in your classroom?

PABLO PICASSO'S SHAPES

 Three Musicians

Pablo Picasso was an artist who liked to use geometric shapes in interesting ways. He left out details so that his artworks did not look like real life. They are **abstract**.

 Self-Portrait with Palette

 Multimedia Biographies
Visit *The Learning Site*
www.harcourtschool.com

C **The Enameled Casserole**

THINK ABOUT ART

Do the people and things in Picasso's paintings look real? Tell why or why not.

portrait
self-portrait

Shapes and People

What shapes do you see in these artworks? A **portrait** shows what a person or a group looks like. In a **self-portrait**, an artist paints himself or herself.

A Luis Jaso,
My Family Before I Was Born

B Antavio,
Student art

Favorite-People Portrait

Think about your family or another group of people you would like to paint.

1. Fold the edges of your paper to make a frame.

2. Draw a group portrait. Paint it. Decorate the frame.

REFLECT

What lines and shapes did you use in your portrait?

Where have you seen portraits? What did they look like?

Unit 1 Review and Reflect

Vocabulary and Concepts

Tell which picture goes best with each item.

1. outline

2. free-form shapes

3. portrait

4. geometric shapes

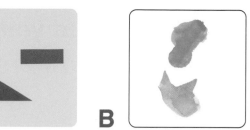

A

B

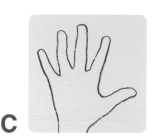

C

D

Tell which picture goes best with each item.

5. lines

6. self-portrait

7. movement

8. organic shapes

E

F

G

H

9. Tell about the lines and shapes in this picture.

Make Inferences

Read pages 30–31 again. Make a chart like this one. Tell what you think about the pictures.

What I See and Read	+ What I Know	= What I Think
The fence has lines.	Fences like this are metal.	This fence is ____.
The leaf is yellow.	Leaves change colors in the fall.	It is ____.

Write About Art

Write sentences to tell what you see and think is happening in the painting *Autumn*.

A woman is feeding six ducks.

Grandma Moses, *Autumn*

▲ Sofonisba Anguissola, *The Chess Game*

LOCATE IT

This painting is in the National Museum in Poznan, Poland.

See Maps of Museums and Art Sites, pages 144–147.

Poland

42

Mix and Match

Friends

Two friends are better than one,

And three are better than two.

And four are much better still.

Just

    think

        what

four friends can do!

Anonymous

Unit Vocabulary

primary colors

secondary colors

warm colors

cool colors

value

tint

shade

mood

seascape

horizon line

ABOUT THE ARTIST

See Gallery of Artists, pages 182–191.

 Multimedia Art Glossary
Visit *The Learning Site*
www.harcourtschool.com

43

Story Elements

A picture can tell a story. Who is in this picture? What are these **characters** doing?

Eric Carle, illustration from *Draw Me a Star* LITERATURE LINK

A story also has a setting. The **setting** is the time and place. Tell about the setting in this artwork.

Read the paragraph. Then make a story map.
Tell a story about the art on page 44.

Men, women, children, and pets are working
together. Someone is in the house. Others are outside
in the garden. It is starting to rain. A man is painting
a rainbow. Maybe this will help stop the rain.

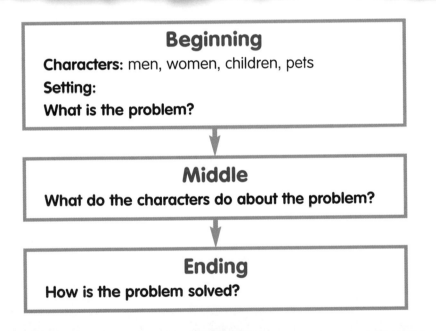

Beginning
Characters: men, women, children, pets
Setting:
What is the problem?

Middle
What do the characters do about the problem?

Ending
How is the problem solved?

On Your Own
Make a story map about the painting
on pages 42–43. Use your map to tell
a story.

Colors Work Together

Can you find a red hat, a yellow shirt, and a blue balloon in this painting? Red, yellow, and blue are **primary colors**. What other colors do you see?

Jonathan Green, *Balloons for a Dime*

Primary colors can be mixed to make the **secondary colors**—orange, green, and violet.

A **color wheel** shows colors in rainbow order.
What two colors make orange? Green? Violet?

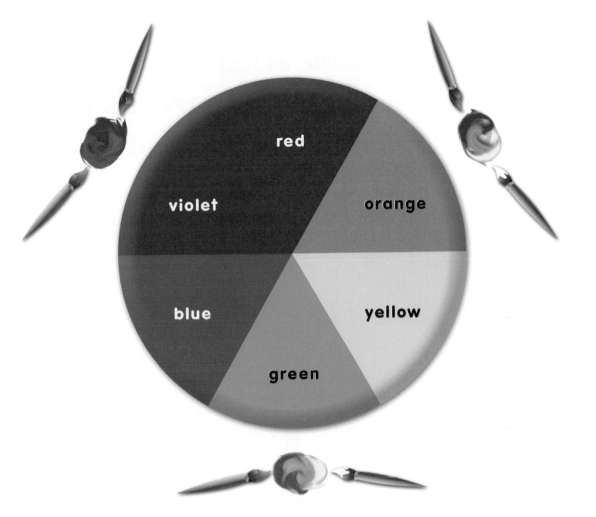

Rainbow Pinwheel

1. Mix colors and paint them in rainbow order.

2. Cut in from each corner. Fold to the middle. Glue.

Warm and Cool Colors

How does each painting make you feel? Colors can make us feel certain ways. Red, orange, and yellow are **warm colors**. Blue, green, and violet are **cool colors**.

Diego Rivera,
La Era

warm colors   cool colors

B   **Claude Monet,**
The Waterlily Pond

Cool colors can help make pictures feel cool and calm. Warm colors give art more energy and can make pictures seem hot.

Artist's Workshop

Mood Painting

Paint a picture of yourself doing your favorite thing. Use mostly warm or cool colors to show how you feel.

49

Georgia O'Keeffe's
Seasons

A *Autumn Leaves,
Lake George, N.Y.*

Georgia O'Keeffe is famous for her paintings of flowers and other objects in nature. She looked closely at them and painted them large. She wanted to show how she felt about the colors.

 Apple Blossoms

Think About Art

How do you feel when you look at these paintings? What colors do you see?

Multimedia Biographies
Visit *The Learning Site*
www.harcourtschool.com

51

Light and Dark Colors

What do these paintings show? Which parts are light colors? The **value** of a color is how light or dark it is.

A   Gustavo, age 7,
Violet Light

B   Suzanne Valadon,
Bouquet and Cat

Make a **tint**, or lighter color, by mixing a color with white. Make a **shade**, or darker color, by mixing a color with black.

Fall Bouquet Painting

PLAN

Think about your favorite flowers.

CREATE

1. **Cut out a vase. Glue it onto a sheet of paper.**

2. **Make tints and shades. Paint many flowers and leaves.**

REFLECT

Which parts of your flowers are light?
Which parts are dark?

Are the colors of your clothes light or dark?

Colors Tell Stories

Many artworks tell a story. What story does this painting tell?

Vincent van Gogh, *First Steps, after Millet*

Tell about the setting in the painting. What colors did the artist mostly use? What **mood**, or feeling, do the colors give?

54

Story Puppet Scene

PLAN . . . .

Brainstorm ideas for a story scene. What is the setting and who are the characters? What mood do you want to show?

CREATE . . . .

1. Draw and cut out characters. Glue them onto craft sticks.

2. Draw and color the setting. Cut a slit. Move your puppets as you tell a story.

REFLECT . . . .

How did you use colors to show mood in your story?

Edna Crawford, Animator

Edna Crawford works on her computer to create cartoon art. She is an **animator**. She makes many pictures of a character until she has one she likes best. It is important to her that her characters seem lifelike.

Apple Surprise

1

2

3

4

5

6

DID YOU KNOW?

When she was young, Edna Crawford painted a big red balloon that looked like an apple. Then she painted a worm on it. In college, this became the idea for her story *Apple Surprise.*

Think About Art

How can you use a computer to make pictures?

Multimedia Biographies
Visit *The Learning Site*
www.harcourtschool.com

Colors in Seascapes

What is going on in this painting? A **seascape** is an artwork that shows a water setting, like the sea. What colors did the artist use to show water? Why?

Winslow Homer, *Gloucester Harbor*

Can you find the line where the sky and the water meet? This is called the **horizon line**.

Crayon-Resist Seascape

PLAN

Think about all the things you can find on the ocean and in the ocean.

CREATE

1. **Draw a horizon line. Use crayons to draw boats. Add plants and animals under the water.**

2. **Paint watercolor over the picture. Make it darker at the bottom.**

REFLECT

What colors did you use? What does the water look like?

Where can you find a seascape in your town?

59

Unit 2 Review and Reflect

Tell which picture goes best with each item.

 A  B  C  D

1. cool colors
2. tint

3. primary colors
4. value

 E  F  G  H

5. shade
6. seascape

7. warm colors
8. secondary colors

9. Tell about the setting of this picture. Point out the horizon line. Tell about the mood.

Winslow Homer, *Gloucester Harbor*

Story Elements

Reread about Edna Crawford on pages 56–57. Think about the story her artwork shows. Fill in the story map.

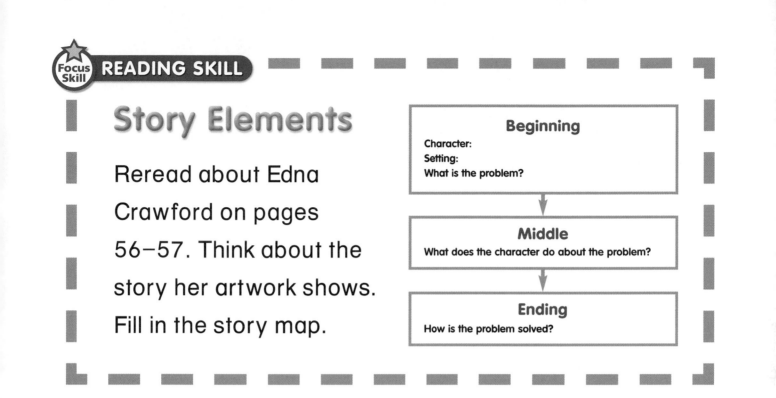

Beginning
Character:
Setting:
What is the problem?

↓

Middle
What does the character do about the problem?

↓

Ending
How is the problem solved?

Write About Art

Write a story about the painting *Balloons for a Dime*.

My friends and I were playing in the park on Saturday.

Jonathan Green, *Balloons for a Dime*

▲ Thomas Hart Benton, *Trail Riders*

LOCATE IT

This painting is in the National Gallery of Art in Washington, D.C.

See Maps of Museums and Art Sites, pages 144–147.

Washington, D.C.

Nature's Way

She'll Be Coming 'Round the Mountain

She'll be coming 'round the mountain
when she comes,
She'll be coming 'round the mountain
when she comes,
She'll be coming 'round the mountain,
She'll be coming 'round the mountain,
She'll be coming 'round the mountain
when she comes.

Traditional Song

Unit Vocabulary

pattern	texture
repetition	weaving
print	visual texture
rhythm	

ABOUT THE ARTIST

See Gallery of Artists, pages 182–191.

Multimedia Art Glossary
Visit *The Learning Site*
www.harcourtschool.com

63

Important Details

What is happening in this picture? What things are blowing in the wind?

Stefano Vitale, cover illustration from *When the Wind Stops,* by Charlotte Zolotow   LITERATURE LINK

When you look closely at a picture, you see **details**, or small parts. Some details are important for showing what a picture is mainly about.

64

Read about the **important details** in the picture on page 64. Add details to the web.

The seasons are changing quickly for a boy and his mother. Spring flowers and fall leaves blow by in the wind. Snowflakes and raindrops do, too. The sun, the moon, and stars float by in the sky.

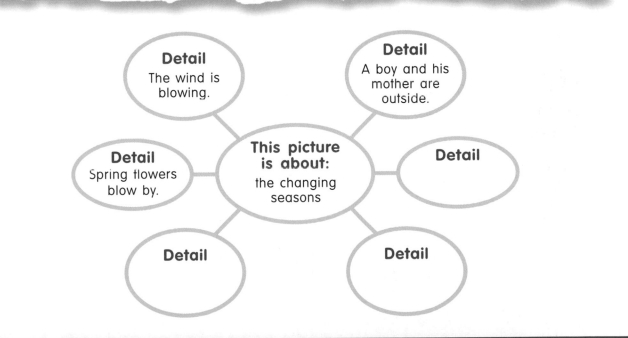

Detail
The wind is blowing.

Detail
A boy and his mother are outside.

Detail
Spring flowers blow by.

This picture is about:
the changing seasons

Detail

Detail

Detail

On Your Own
Look again at pages 62–63. What details do you see? Make a web that shows the important details.

Lesson
11

Vocabulary

pattern
repetition

Shapes Make Patterns

What does each artwork show? What
shapes make up the big star in the quilt?

A

**Unknown artist,
Star of
Bethlehem quilt**

Point to the arms of the star and to the flowers.
Name the shapes—*triangle, flower, triangle, flower.*
Repeating shapes, lines, or colors make a **pattern**.

Every pattern has **repetition**, or repeating parts. What repetition does this art show? What comes next in the flag pattern?

 Jasper Johns,
Three Flags

Patterned Picture Frame

Fold up and glue the edges of your paper to make a frame. Decorate with a pattern of shapes.

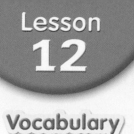

Colors Make Patterns

What do the artworks show? Point to and say the colors that make up each pattern.

 A Unknown artist, Guaymí necklace

B Heather, grade 2, *Fish Print*

Each fish in artwork **B** looks the same. Each is a **print**, or a copy of an artwork. One way to make a print is to cut out a shape. Press the shape into paint and then onto paper over and over.

Patterned Stand-Up Animal

 PLAN

Think about the shape of your favorite animal.

 CREATE

1. Fold a large sheet of paper in half. Draw and cut out an animal.

2. Cut out one shape a few times from a sponge or cardboard. Print a pattern of colors.

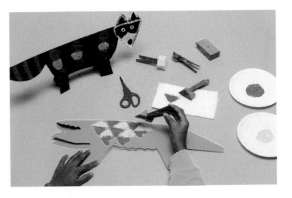

REFLECT

What patterns did you make?

What color patterns do you see around you?

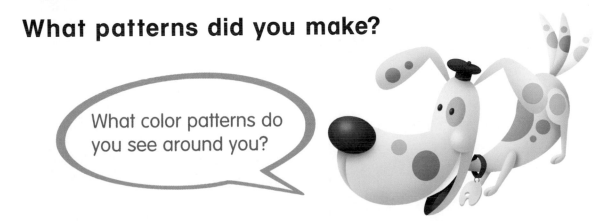

EGYPTIAN ART

A Gold mask of Tutankhamen

Many of Egypt's most famous artworks were made long ago for kings and queens. The gold mask of young King Tutankhamen was found in his tomb in a pyramid. What patterns do you see?

An artist made this hippo long ago. It is decorated with pictures of plants from the Nile River in Egypt where hippos live.

DID YOU KNOW?

The pyramids at Giza are one of the seven wonders of the ancient world. They are the oldest and largest stone structures on Earth.

THINK ABOUT ART

Why do you think ancient Egyptian artworks are still famous today?

C Pyramids at Giza

Patterns Show Rhythm

What do you see in these artworks? Follow the monkeys' path from the trees to the ground. Can you find the same pattern of movement in artwork **B**?

B Unknown artist, Peruvian textile

Henri Rousseau, *Exotic Landscape*

In most art, your eyes will follow a pattern of colors, lines, or shapes. This movement that comes from patterns is called **rhythm**.

Rain Forest Scene

PLAN

Imagine a rain forest with things moving in it. What patterns could you use to show this?

CREATE

1. Color trees and other plants. Make patterns with things like flowers, leaves, and tree trunks.

2. Add a pattern of animals moving across the picture. Give your picture a strong rhythm.

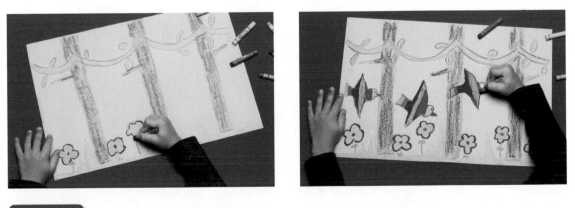

REFLECT

What patterns did you use? What is the rhythm of your artwork?

Patterns and Textures in Weavings

How would this artwork feel if you could touch it—soft, scratchy, bumpy? The way something feels is its **texture**.

Nancy Curry,
Riverdance

This **weaving** is an artwork made by putting paper strips and other things over and under each other. What is the pattern of this weaving?

Found Object Weaving

PLAN

Think about patterns and textures you would like to put in a weaving.

CREATE

1. **Wrap yarn around a piece of cardboard to make a loom.**

2. **Weave things like paper strips, ribbons, vines, and grass. Add found objects.**

REFLECT

What patterns and textures does your weaving have?

What different textures are you wearing?

JACOB LAWRENCE'S PATTERNS

Jacob Lawrence liked to tell stories through his paintings. He used patterns of shapes to help tell his stories. What are the people here doing? How do your eyes move around each painting? Why?

 The Street

What patterns and rhythms can you find in *Vaudeville*?

B   *Vaudeville*

THINK ABOUT ART

What story do you think Jacob Lawrence is telling in each painting?

Multimedia Biographies
Visit *The Learning Site*
www.harcourtschool.com

77

Patterns Show Texture

How are these artworks alike and different?
What do you think each animal feels like?

A   **Ann Hanson,**
Dancing Lizard Couple

B   **Albrecht Dürer,**
Hare

Texture we can see but not touch is called
visual texture. Patterns of lines, colors, or
shapes are used to show how things could feel.

Textured Animal Rubbing

PLAN

Think about textures some animals have, like bumpy skin, smooth scales, and soft wool.

CREATE

1. Use two large pieces of paper. Cut the outline of an animal.

2. Put textures under your paper. Rub with a crayon. Stuff with paper and staple.

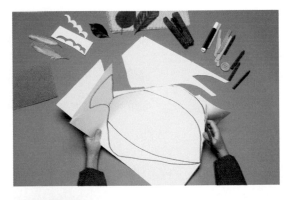 

REFLECT

What textures did you show?
How did you make them?

79

Unit 3 Review and Reflect

Vocabulary and Concepts

Tell which picture goes best with each word.

1. weaving

2. print

3. pattern

4. visual texture

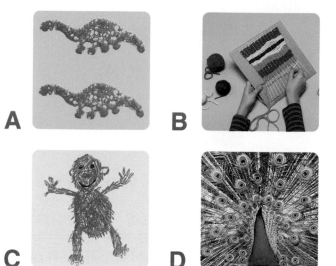

A   B

C   D

. . . .

5. Describe the textures you would feel if you could touch this animal.

6. Tell about the repetition you see in this picture.

7. Tell about the rhythm in the picture.

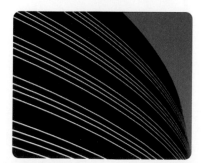

Important Details

Reread about the Egyptian hippo on page 71. Write important details in a web.

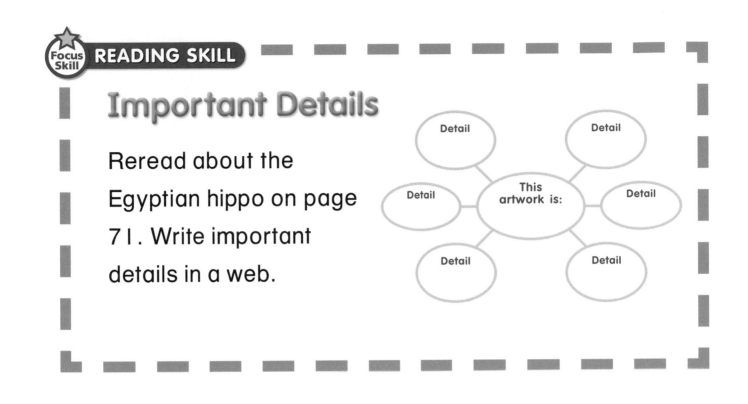

- Detail
- Detail
- Detail
- This artwork is:
- Detail
- Detail
- Detail

Write About Art

Write a paragraph to describe important details about the lizards. Tell about the colors, shapes, patterns, and textures they have.

These dancing lizards have a pattern of pointy white scales going down their backs.

Ann Hanson, *Dancing Lizard Couple*

▲ Glenna Goodacre, *Olympic Wannabes*

LOCATE IT

This sculpture is in Selby Five Points Park in Sarasota, Florida.

See Maps of Museums and Art Sites, pages 144–147.

Sarasota, FL

Surprises Everywhere

At the Top of My Voice

When I stamp

The ground thunders,

When I shout

The world rings,

When I sing

The air wonders

How I do such things.

Felice Holman

Unit Vocabulary

form	architecture
sculpture	architect
space	landscape
relief sculpture	foreground
	background

ABOUT THE ARTIST

See Gallery of Artists, pages 182–191.

Multimedia Art Glossary
Visit *The Learning Site*
www.harcourtschool.com

83

Compare and Contrast

When you **compare**, you tell how things are alike. When you **contrast**, you tell how things are different.

A   Horus Falcon

B   Amos Supuni, *Baby Chick*

Compare and contrast these artworks. How are their shapes, colors, patterns, and textures the same? How are they different?

Read the paragraph. Then make a Venn diagram to tell how the artworks are alike and different. Add your own ideas.

Artworks from different places and times may be alike in some ways but different in others. Both of these artworks are birds. Both have patterns of feathers and are made from rock. One difference is that the baby chick from Zimbabwe is flapping its wings. The Egyptian falcon is sitting still.

DIFFERENT
Horus Falcon

sitting still

ALIKE
birds
made from rock

DIFFERENT
Baby Chick

flapping its wings

On Your Own
Fill in a Venn diagram to compare and contrast sculptures of two children on pages 82–83.

Shapes and Forms

How are these artworks alike? How are they different? Each artwork has **form**— or height, width, and depth.

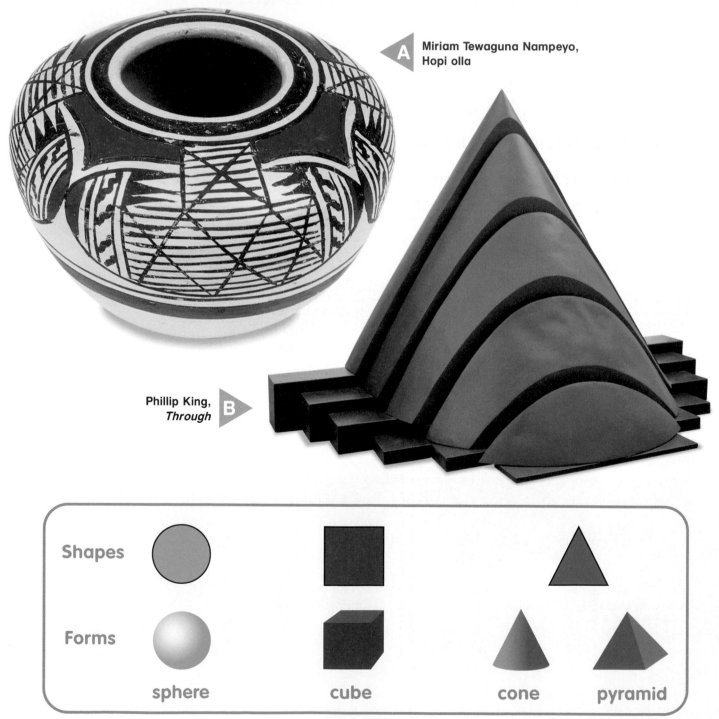

A Miriam Tewaguna Nampeyo, Hopi olla

Phillip King, *Through* B

Shapes			
Forms	sphere	cube	cone	pyramid

Decorated Clay Bowl

 PLAN

Think about how to decorate a clay bowl.

CREATE

1. **Roll clay into a ball. Push in with your thumbs. Pinch up the sides.**

2. **Smooth the sides. Make patterns. Paint it when it's dry.**

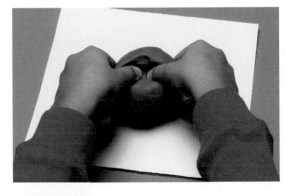

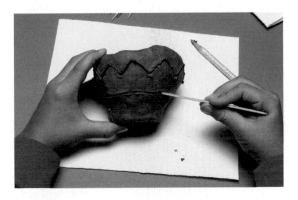

REFLECT

What form was the clay when you started? How did the form change?

What forms do you see in your classroom?

Sculpted Forms

What forms do these artworks show? Each of these artworks is a **sculpture**, an artwork that you can see from all sides.

 Gerhard Marcks, *The Bremen Town Musicians*

 Deborah Butterfield, *Aluminum Horse #5*

The part of an artwork that is not filled in is called **space**. Find the space around, through, and between the animals in the sculptures.

Foil Sculpture

 PLAN ....

Think of an animal sculpture you want to make.

CREATE ....

1. **Crumple, pinch, and pull foil to make the body and the head.**

2. **Crumple more foil onto the body. Add legs, a tail, ears, or wings.**

 REFLECT ....

Where do you find space in your sculpture?

Tell about space in your classroom.

Cowboys and Cowgirls in Art

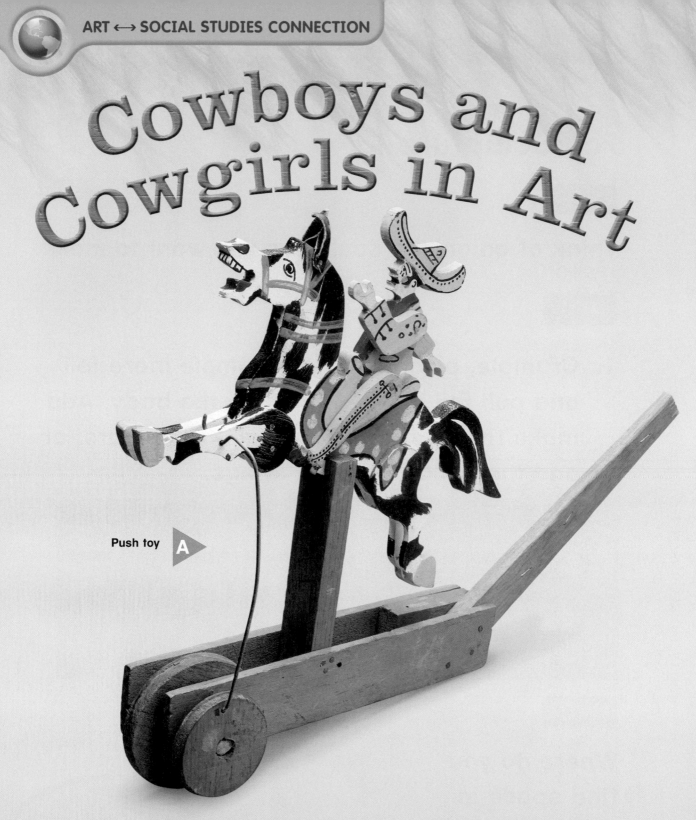

Push toy A

Cowboys and cowgirls are known for riding horses well. This toy shows a Mexican cowboy, or *charro*. What shapes and forms did the toymaker use? What colors and patterns do you see?

90

Artists made these things. How are they works of art? How might each one be used?

Sam Garrett's Western boots **C**

B Buckeye Blake, *Fanny Sperry Steele*

Think About Art

What does this art tell you about the life of cowboys and cowgirls?

Relief Sculpture

In a **relief sculpture**, forms stand out from a flat surface. What do you see happening in this relief sculpture?

Unknown artist, Scenes from the life of a child

This artwork shows important times in a child's life. How do you think the artist made the forms stand out? Tell where you see space.

Clay Tile Relief Sculpture

PLAN

What is something interesting about you? Think of a picture to show it, such as a fish if you like fishing.

CREATE

1. Make your clay flat. Draw your picture on the clay.

2. Make the picture stand out. Use tools to carve and take away parts.

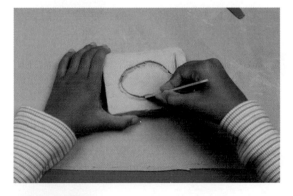

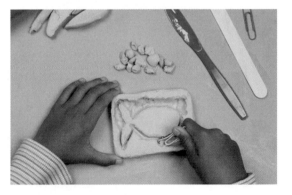

REFLECT

What forms did you show in your artwork? Why? How did you use space?

Look at a coin. How is it like your relief sculpture?

Architecture

How are the buildings alike and different? **Architecture** is the art and science of planning buildings and other structures. An **architect** is a person who plans what they will look like.

A *Neuschwanstein Castle*, Germany

What lines, shapes, and forms did the architects use in these buildings? How do they look like things in nature?

 I. M. Pei,
Pyramids at the Louvre

Amazing School Model

1. **Make a model of an amazing school.**

2. **Decorate it. Add a sign.**

Frank Lloyd Wright's

Frank Lloyd Wright was a famous architect. He designed buildings so they would blend in with the land around them. *Fallingwater* is a house he designed to let a stream and waterfall flow under it.

A Exterior of *Fallingwater*

Buildings

B *Solomon R. Guggenheim Museum*

C Frank Lloyd Wright standing beside an architectural model

Think About Art

What forms did Frank Lloyd Wright use? How did he use space?

Multimedia Biographies
Visit *The Learning Site*
www.harcourtschool.com

landscape
foreground
background

Landscapes

What do you see in these artworks? A **landscape** shows an outdoor scene of the land. The part of the art that is large and seems nearest to you is the **foreground**.

A Claude Monet,
In the Meadow

The part of the art that looks small and seems farthest away is the **background**.

Kacy, grade 2,
Student art B

Kacy

3-D Landscape Painting

PLAN

Imagine a beautiful landscape scene.

CREATE

1. Paint a landscape with a clear horizon line.

2. Make things large in the foreground and small in the background.

REFLECT

What is in the foreground of your landscape? How do you know? Where is the horizon line?

Unit 4 Review and Reflect

Vocabulary and Concepts

Choose the best answer to finish each sentence.

1. A picture of the outdoors is a _____.

   A architecture
   B form
   C sculpture
   D landscape

2. An _____ plans buildings.

   A background
   B architect
   C foreground
   D architecture

Choose the word from the box that best completes each sentence.

architecture
background
foreground
form
relief sculpture
sculpture
space

3. The part of an artwork that is empty is called _____.

4. The part of a picture that seems farthest from you is the _____.

5. You can walk all around a _____.

6. A cube is not flat. It is a _____.

7. A sculpture that stands out from a flat surface is a _____.

8. The part of a picture that seems closest to you is the _____.

9. The art of planning buildings is _____.

Compare and Contrast

Reread about Frank Lloyd Wright's buildings on pages 96–97. Make a Venn diagram to compare and contrast *Fallingwater* and the Guggenheim Museum.

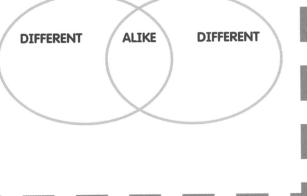

DIFFERENT   ALIKE   DIFFERENT

Write About Art

Write a paragraph to compare and contrast two animals from *The Bremen Town Musicians*. First tell how they are alike. Then tell how they are different.

 A cat and a
donkey are alike in
some ways but are
also very different.

Gerhard Marcks, *The Bremen Town Musicians*

▲ Pieter Brueghel the Elder, *The Hay Harvest*

 **LOCATE IT**

This painting is in the National Gallery in Prague, Czech Republic.

See Maps of Museums and Art Sites, pages 144–147.

Czech Republic

Good Neighbors

Harvest Breeze

The smell of fresh cut hay
Aloft on the harvest breeze
Sneaking up from field to house
Up the pasture through the trees.

Tim Gallagher

Unit Vocabulary

emphasis   contrast
subject   textiles
balance   designs
symmetry

ABOUT THE ARTIST

See Gallery of Artists,
pages 182–191.

Multimedia Art Glossary
Visit *The Learning Site*
www.harcourtschool.com

Main Idea

The most important idea of a paragraph, a story, or an artwork is the **main idea**.

Paul Gauguin, *Breton Girls Dancing, Pont-Aven*

What is the main idea of this painting? Use details about the people, the place, and the action to figure out what it is mostly about.

Read the paragraph. Then make a diagram. Use the details to help you figure out the main idea.

Three girls are having fun doing a folk dance. They are in a field, holding hands and doing dance steps. They are wearing long dresses, hats, and wooden shoes. The girls look as if they all know the dance and enjoy doing it.

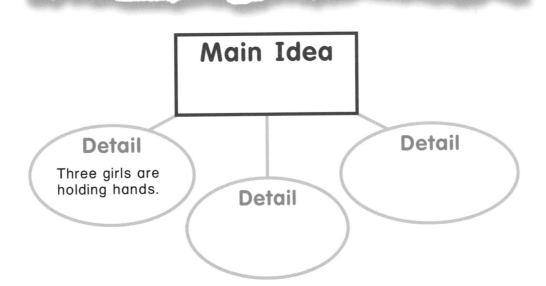

Main Idea

Detail
Three girls are holding hands.

Detail

Detail

On Your Own

What are the different groups of people doing in the painting on pages 102–103? What is the main idea?

Emphasis Using Color

What do you see first in each painting?
Why?

A **Henri Matisse,**
Goldfish

B **Ichiryusai Hiroshige,**
Macaw on a Pine Branch

Artists can use color to help you notice a
certain part of an artwork. Making things stand
out is called **emphasis**.

"Around the Town" Painting

PLAN ....

Think of places you like in your neighborhood.

CREATE ....

1. **Fold your paper two times. Cut a V on the top to make a roof. Unfold.**

2. **Paint places from your neighborhood. Use color to give emphasis to your *favorite* place.**

REFLECT ....

How did you use color to make your favorite place stand out?

Where do you see color emphasis in your classroom?

Emphasis Using Size

What is happening in each artwork? What is the most important thing you see?

 A Katsushika Hokusai,
The Great Wave off Kanagawa

What an artwork is about is called the **subject**. Artists often make the subject large for emphasis.

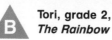 **B** Tori, grade 2,
The Rainbow

108

Found Object Collage

 PLAN ·

Think about something real or make-believe you can make with found objects.

CREATE ·

1. Glue objects onto paper. Make one part stand out.

2. Draw, paint, and decorate the background.

REFLECT ·

How did you make the subject of your picture stand out?

Where do you see size emphasis in your classroom?

Famous Photographers

A **photographer** is an artist who takes pictures with a camera. Ansel Adams is well known for his black-and-white photographs of landscapes. Where do you see the light in *Moon Over Half Dome*?

A Ansel Adams photographing the Big Sur coast

Ansel Adams, *Moon Over Half Dome* **B**

110

Flor Garduño is
best known for her
photographs of people.
This photograph shows
a celebration of light.

 Flor Garduño,
Basket of Light

D Flor Garduño
photographing a volcano

Think
About Art

How does a
photographer use
light and size to
show emphasis?

Balance Using Shapes

What do these artworks show? The artists put the same shapes on both sides. These artworks have **balance**.

A Ancient Greek black-figure hydria with women running

B Turkish plate decorated with flame motif

Lay your pencil on each artwork to divide it in half. Each artwork has **symmetry** since both sides are the same. How is the symmetry in **A** different from **B**?

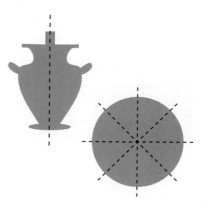

Sun Print

PLAN ....

Think of things from nature that have two sides the same, like a butterfly or a flower.

CREATE ....

1. Fold paper. Cut out a shape. Lay it on dark paper. Put it in the sun.

2. Take off the shape to see the sun print. Decorate it with a balanced design.

REFLECT ....

How did the sun make a print? How does your picture show balance and symmetry?

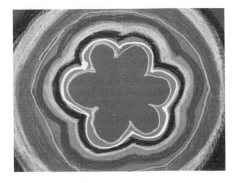

Balance Using Color

What do you see in each painting? How are the two sides of painting **A** alike?

 Edgar Degas,
Two Dancers in Blue Costumes

Artists often put the same color on both sides of an artwork to balance it. Artists also use things that are very different, like light and dark colors, to show **contrast**.

Rembrandt van Rijn,
Members of the Drapers Club (Staalmeesters)

Contrast helps you notice things like the men's faces. What makes this painting balanced?

Famous-Person Portrait

1. Draw a portrait of a famous person.

2. Color the background so that it shows balance and contrast.

Frida Kahlo's

Frida Kahlo is famous for her self-portraits. As a teenager in Mexico, she was in an accident. While Frida rested in bed, she taught herself to paint. She looked in a mirror and painted many portraits of herself, showing her ideas and feelings.

A *The Frame, Self-Portrait*

Portraits

DID YOU KNOW?

Frida Kahlo liked to include the flowers and animals of Mexico in her art. Tell where she used these things to balance her self-portrait on page 116.

B Photograph of Frida Kahlo

C *Frida and Diego Rivera*

Think
About Art

What is special about you that you would put in a self-portrait?

Multimedia Biographies
Visit *The Learning Site*
www.harcourtschool.com

Art to Wear

What do you notice about these artworks? Some artists use **textiles**, or cloth and other fibers, to make beautiful clothing.

Ceremonial clothing of King Mbop Mbine A

B Child's blouse with geometric mola

Pictures and patterns on artworks are called **designs**. What patterns do you see on the clothing? How are the designs balanced?

Celebration Vest

PLAN

Think about a celebration where you could wear a decorated vest.

CREATE

1. Make a vest from a paper bag. Cut a slit up the front. Cut holes for your head and arms.

2. Decorate your vest. Think about balance and emphasis. Glue on objects. Add some weaving.

REFLECT

How is the design of your vest balanced?

Unit 5 Review and Reflect

Choose the best answer to finish each sentence.

1. Light and dark colors create _____.

   A textiles
   B symmetry
   C contrast
   D subject

2. Making something stand out in an artwork is _____.

   A emphasis
   B balance
   C textiles
   D designs

3. If both sides are exactly alike, art has _____.

   A symmetry
   B contrast
   C subject
   D emphasis

4. What an artwork is about is the _____.

   A symmetry
   B contrast
   C balance
   D subject

5. An artwork with the same shapes on both sides has _____.

   A textiles
   B balance
   C subject
   D emphasis

6. Cloth and fabric are _____.

   A balance
   B emphasis
   C designs
   D textiles

Main Idea

Reread about Frida Kahlo on page 116. Look at the art. Then make a diagram to tell the main idea and details.

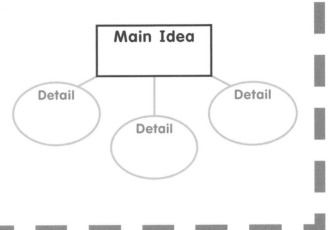

Write About Art

Write a paragraph that tells the main idea of the painting. Make a diagram like the one above, and use ideas from it as you write.

Sometimes giant waves form in the ocean.

Katsushika Hokusai, *The Great Wave off Kanagawa*

▲ Aztec feather headdress

LOCATE IT

This headdress is in the Museum of Ethnology in Vienna, Austria.

See Maps of Museums and Art Sites, pages 144–147.

Austria

World Treasures

Happy Thought

The world is so full of a
number of things,
I'm sure we should all be
as happy as kings.

Robert Louis Stevenson

Unit Vocabulary

mosaic	variety
unity	story cloth
symbol	graphic art
still life	

Multimedia Art Glossary
Visit *The Learning Site*
www.harcourtschool.com

Cause and Effect

What is happening to make the girl cover her ears in this painting? The **cause** is the reason something happens. The **effect** is what happens.

Norman Rockwell, *The Music Man*

Read. Then make a chart. Tell the cause and the effects that happen because of it.

My brother loves to sing cowboy songs, but he sings them too loudly. He sings so hard and so loudly that his feet come off the ground. Our dog starts to howl, and I have to cover my ears.

Effect The dog howls.

Cause
The girl's brother is singing too loudly.

Effect

Effect

On Your Own
Choose one of the stamps on pages 138–139. Make a cause-and-effect chart to tell about it.

Mosaics

What do these pictures show? A **mosaic** is an artwork made with small pieces of things like stone, tile, glass, or paper.

 Unknown artist,
Rabbit Devouring a Bunch of Grapes

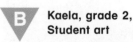 Kaela, grade 2,
Student art

When all parts look as if they belong together, the artwork has **unity**. How does each mosaic show unity?

126

Paper-Plate Mosaic

PLAN

Think of a mosaic design for a plate. What patterns or subject will you show?

CREATE

1. Draw a picture. Cut or tear paper and foil into small pieces.

2. Glue the pieces onto the plate to make shapes and patterns.

REFLECT

How does your mosaic show unity?

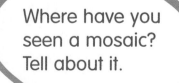
Where have you seen a mosaic? Tell about it.

Designs of Money

A **symbol** is a person or thing that stands for something else. Who is George Washington? What does he stand for?

 A One-dollar bill, U.S., front

 B One-dollar bill, U.S., back

C Farthings, England

D Twenty peso bill, Mexico

What pictures and symbols do you see on the money? What do you think the symbols tell about the countries?

How do the coins and bills show unity? Where do you see balance? Emphasis?

E 1000-yen bill, Japan

F Gold panda coin, China

Gold kangaroo coin, Australia G

Artist's Workshop

Money Design

1. Choose a symbol for your city or state.

2. Design a coin or a bill. Make prints.

Mary Cassatt's Treasures

Mary Cassatt was an American artist who lived most of her life in France. She is best known for her paintings of mothers and children. Cassatt liked to show people in everyday activities. She used light, bright colors in her art.

A

Women Admiring a Child

How did Cassatt use lines, shapes, and colors to unify her art?

B *Portrait of the Artist*

Multimedia Biographies
Visit *The Learning Site*
www.harcourtschool.com

Think About Art

What everyday activities would you like to paint? Why?

C *Summertime*

Still Lifes

What objects are in each painting? A group of objects arranged by an artist and then shown in an artwork is a **still life**.

 William H. Johnson,
Still Life—Fruit, Bottles

Jacob van Hulsdonck,
A Still Life of Fruit and Flowers in a Basket B

An artwork with different things in it has **variety**. What lines, shapes, colors, and textures are in each still life? How does each show unity?

Still-Life Painting

 PLAN

Arrange a variety of objects in interesting ways. Put some objects in front of others.

CREATE

1. Choose the best arrangement and draw it.

2. Paint light areas first. Then paint darker areas.

REFLECT

What lines, shapes, colors, and textures are in your still life?

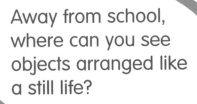

Away from school, where can you see objects arranged like a still life?

Stories in Cloth Art

What is happening in this piece of art? A **story cloth** is an old form of artwork that tells a story on cloth or other textiles.

Unknown artist, Hmong story cloth of village life

What can you tell about the life of these people from this artwork?

Story-Cloth Collage

PLAN

Think about a favorite memory and the story it tells.

CREATE

1. Draw important parts of your story on cloth or paper.

2. Glue cloth and objects onto the picture. Make a border.

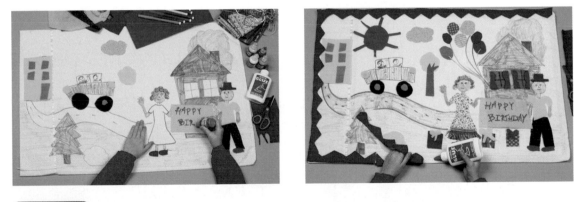

REFLECT

How does your story cloth tell the most important parts of your story?

What other cloth art have you seen? Did it tell a story?

135

Gerald McDermott,

BOOK ILLUSTRATOR

Gerald McDermott is a storyteller and artist for children's books. He began studying art when he was four years old. In *Coyote* he uses bright colors and patterns to tell a trickster tale.

136

Think About Art

What do you think is happening on this page of the story? Why?

Art on Stamps

Which of these stamps is your favorite?
Why? Stamp designs are examples of
graphic art—art used on products.

A Ashley, *Dog Stamp*—U.S.

B Olympic Soccer—
Ghana, Africa

D *Greetings from Texas*—U.S.

C Beetle—Nicaragua

Some people buy or collect stamps because
of the art. You can also see graphic art on
money, signs, TV ads, and websites.

What are the subjects of these stamps? What stories do some of these artworks tell? How do the stamps show unity and variety?

E Two cowboys—Poland

F *Heroes*—U.S.

Artist's Workshop

Stamp of the Future

1. Draw a stamp that shows the future.

2. Add color. Give your stamp a title.

Unit 6 Review and Reflect

Choose the best answer to complete each sentence.

1. A _____ stands for something.

   A graphic art
   B symbol
   C variety
   D still life

2. An artwork with small pieces of paper glued together is a _____.

   A variety
   B mosaic
   C symbol
   D unity

3. An artwork with many different kinds of things in it has _____.

   A mosaic
   B symbol
   C still life
   D variety

4. A painting of flowers in a vase is a _____.

   A story cloth
   B graphic art
   C still life
   D mosaic

5. An artwork with parts that all belong together has _____.

   A unity
   B story cloth
   C graphic art
   D still life

6. Textiles are used to make a _____.

   A still life
   B mosaic
   C story cloth
   D symbol

Cause and Effect

Reread page 130. Then look at *Women Admiring a Child*. Make a cause-and-effect chart. Tell what is happening and why.

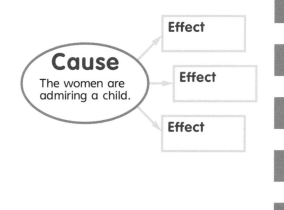

Cause
The women are admiring a child.

Effect

Effect

Effect

Write About Art

Write a cause-and-effect paragraph about the painting *Summertime*. Tell what the people are doing on the boat and why.

> A mother and daughter wanted to have fun, so they went to the lake.

Mary Cassatt, *Summertime*

Student Handbook

CONTENTS

10 Museums and Art Sites
United States

CANADA

WASHINGTON

OREGON

MONTANA

NORTH DAKOTA

MINNESOTA

WISCONSIN

IDAHO

Minneapolis ⑦

SOUTH DAKOTA

WYOMING

IOWA

San Francisco

① NEBRASKA

NEVADA

UTAH

COLORADO

KANSAS

MISSOURI

CALIFORNIA

Santa Fe ⑤

Oklahoma City ③

ARKANSAS

ARIZONA

NEW MEXICO

OKLAHOMA

ALASKA

TEXAS

LOUISIANA

San Antonio ⑧

MEXICO

HAWAII

Use the Electronic Art Gallery CD-ROM, Primary, to locate artworks from other museums and art sites.

LOCATE IT

See art for each of these sites on the pages shown.

1. **Birthplace of Ansel Adams,** page 110

2. **Birthplace of Jasper Johns,** page 67

3. **Cowboy and Western Heritage Museum,** page 91

4. **Eric Carle Museum of Picture Book Art,** page 44

5. **Former home of Georgia O'Keeffe,** page 50

6. **Location of Frank Lloyd Wright's Fallingwater,** page 96

7. **Minneapolis Institute of Art,** page 106

8. **San Antonio Museum of Art,** page 67

9. **Selby Five Points Park,** page 82

10. **The Bennington Museum,** page 22

145

10 Museums and Art Sites
World

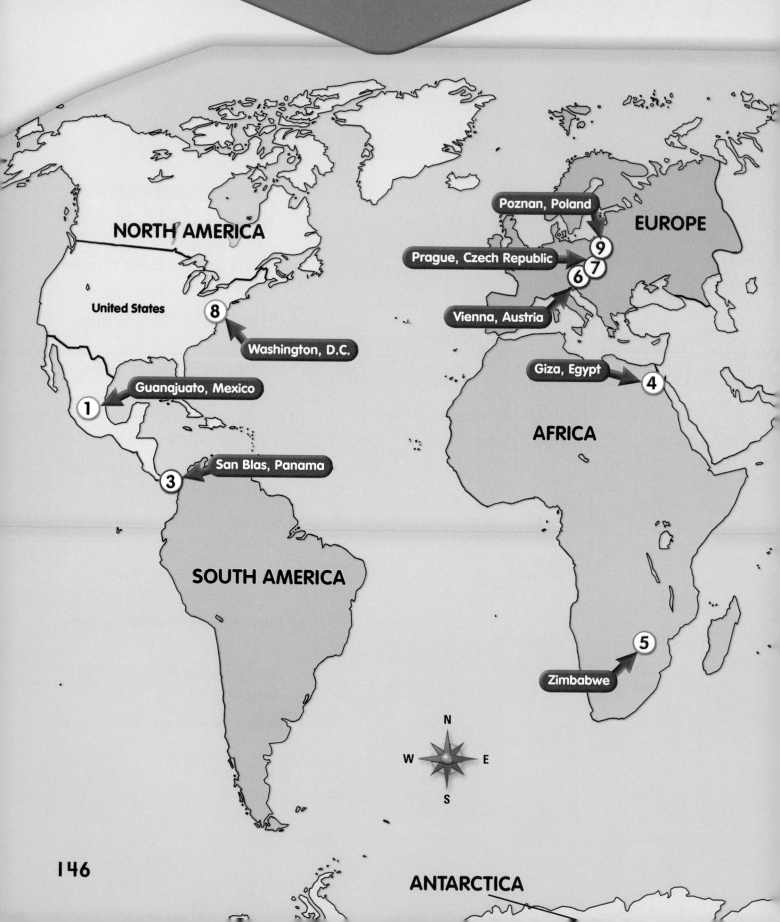

NORTH AMERICA

EUROPE

Poznan, Poland **9**

Prague, Czech Republic **7**
6

United States **8**

Washington, D.C.

Vienna, Austria

Guanajuato, Mexico **1**

Giza, Egypt **4**

AFRICA

San Blas, Panama **3**

SOUTH AMERICA

5

Zimbabwe

N
W   E
S

ANTARCTICA

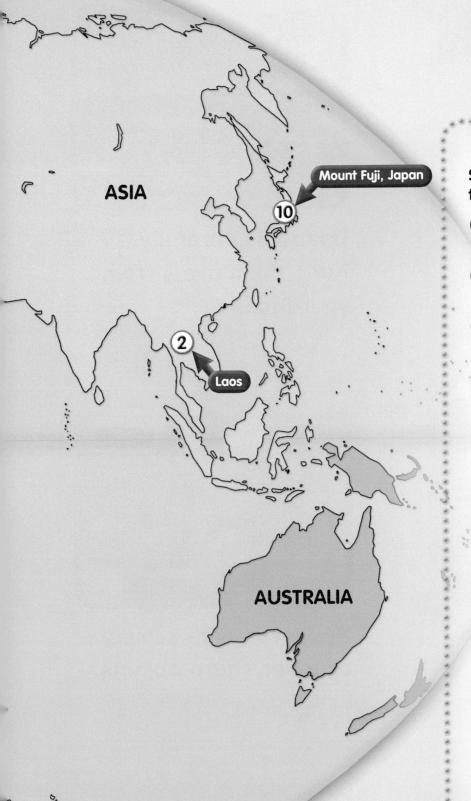

ASIA

Mount Fuji, Japan

10

2

Laos

AUSTRALIA

LOCATE IT

See art for each of these sites on the pages shown.

Art Safety

Use only materials your teacher says are safe.

Use tools carefully. Keep them away from your face.

Wear a smock when you use messy materials.

Never run with scissors or other sharp objects.

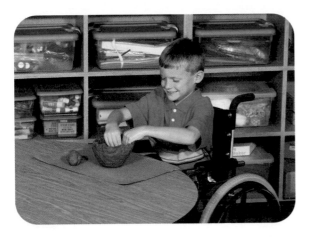

Keep art materials out of your mouth.

Clean up spills right away.

Keep the area around you neat.

Wash your hands after making art.

Art Techniques

DRAWING
Pencil

Press lightly to make light lines.

Press harder to make dark lines.

Tilt the tip to make thick lines.

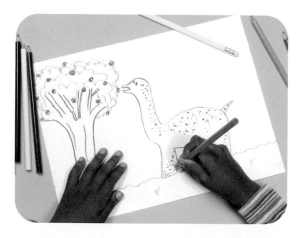

Make dots with the tip.

DRAWING
Markers

You can make dots and circles.

Make thin lines with the tip.

Use the side to make thick lines.

Put the cap on when you are done.

DRAWING
Crayons

Make thin lines and
dots with the tip.

Tilt the tip to make
thick lines.

Make big dots with
the bottom.

Color big spaces with
the side.

DRAWING
Oil Pastels

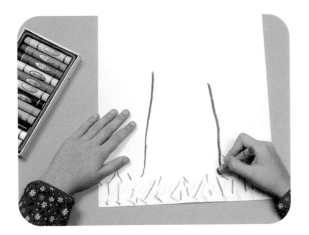

Make light and dark lines.

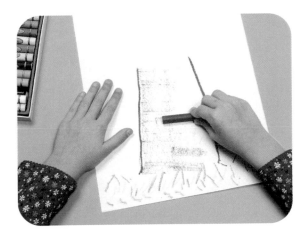

Color big spaces with the side.

Blend colors with a paper towel.

Add colors on top of other colors.

PAINTING
Mixing Colors

1. Dip the brush in a color. Put the paint on a plate or tray.

2. Rinse the brush. Blot. Dip it into another color.

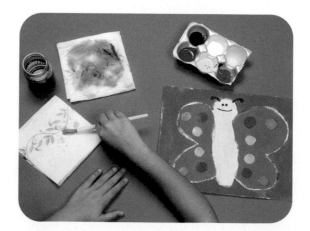

3. Mix the colors. Use the new color.

4. Rinse and blot between colors.

PAINTING
Tempera

Use a wide brush
for thick lines and
big spaces.

Use a thin brush
for details.

Try making short, fast
strokes.

Try holding your brush
different ways. See
what kinds of lines
you can make.

PAINTING
Watercolor

1. Drip water onto each color. Get paint on the brush.

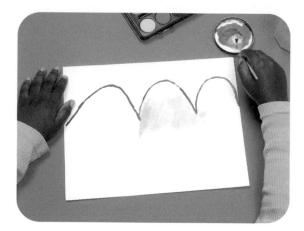

2. Mix colors on a tray or plate.

Press hard to make thick lines. Press lightly to make thin lines.

Paint on wet paper. Make a wash.

PAINTING
Crayon Resist

1. Draw with crayons or oil pastels.

2. Color the picture. Press hard.

3. Paint over the drawing with watercolors.

4. The drawing shows through.

CLAY
Pinch Pot

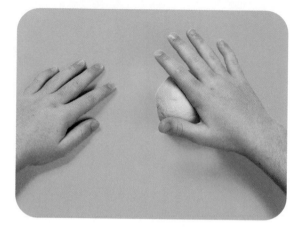

1. Roll clay into a ball.

2. Push down in the middle with your thumbs.

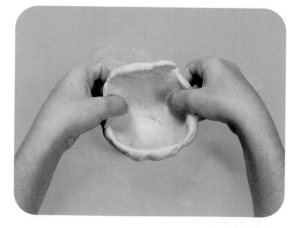

3. Pull up the sides. Try to make them even.

4. Smooth out the sides.

CLAY
Sculpture

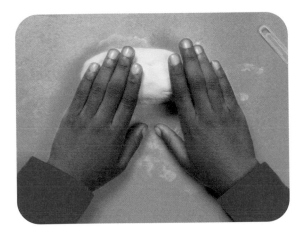

1. Roll clay into an oval.

2. Pull out a part for the head.

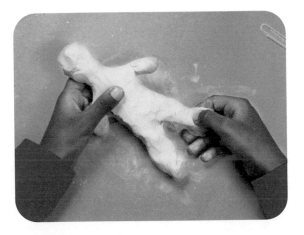

3. Pull out parts for the arms and legs. Make the legs thick.

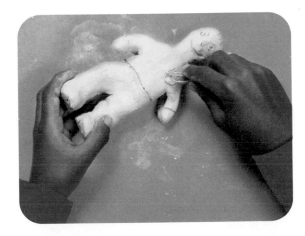

4. Smooth out the sculpture. Add details.

PRINTMAKING
Sponge Prints

1. Cut shapes from a sponge.

2. Wet the sponge. Dip it in paint.

3. Press onto paper.

4. Use a new sponge for each color.

PRINTMAKING
Stencils

1. Draw shapes on thick paper.

2. Cut them out from the inside.

Paint inside the stencil with a brush.

Paint inside the stencil with a sponge.

PRINTMAKING
Foam Tray Prints

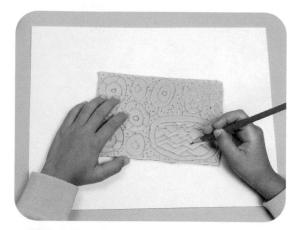

1. Draw on a tray with a pencil. Press hard.

2. Roll on a little ink or paint.

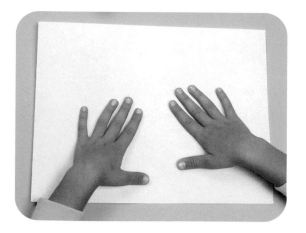

3. Press paper over the tray.

4. Carefully lift the paper.

PRINTMAKING
Monoprint

1. Paint on paper or plastic.

2. Lay paper over the painting.

3. Press the paper onto the painting.

4. Carefully lift off the paper.

WEAVING
Paper Loom

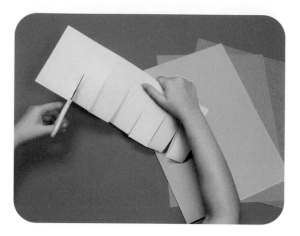

1. Fold paper in half. Cut wide slits.

2. Cut strips of paper.

3. Weave under and over.

4. Continue to weave over and under.

WEAVING
Paper Plate Loom

1. Cut slits in a paper plate.

2. Wrap yarn in the slits.

3. Start in the middle.

4. Weave around, going over and under.

COLLAGE
Mixed Media

1. Cut or tear paper.

2. Use cloth, ribbons, and found objects.

3. Place the things where you want them.

4. Glue.

MOSAIC
Paper

1. Cut or tear paper into pieces.

2. Place the pieces. Make a picture or pattern.

3. Leave small spaces between the pieces.

4. Glue.

PAPER FOLDING
How to Make a Square

1. Start with a rectangle.

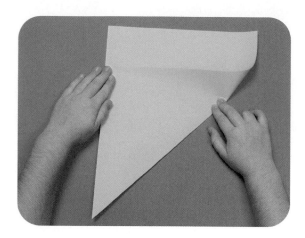

2. Fold the long side. Make the edges touch.

3. Draw a pencil line. Cut along the line.

4. Open.

PAPER FOLDING
3-D Paper Forms
Cones

1. Start with a circle. Cut to the middle.

2. Fold one part under the cut. Tape or glue.

Paper Strip Forms

Fold paper back and forth. Shape into forms.

Bend paper into rounded forms.

Line

thin ▼

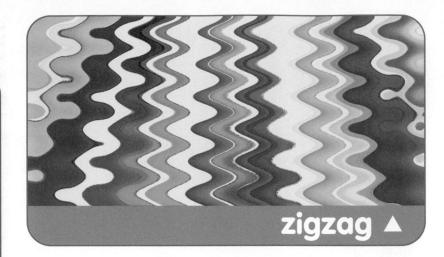
zigzag ▲

curved ▲

thick ▲

diagonal ▼
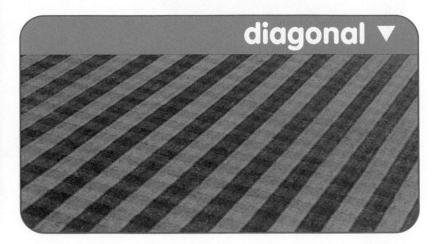

Shape

oval ▲

rectangle ▲

free form ▼

triangle ▼

YIELD

square ▲

organic ▼

Color and Value

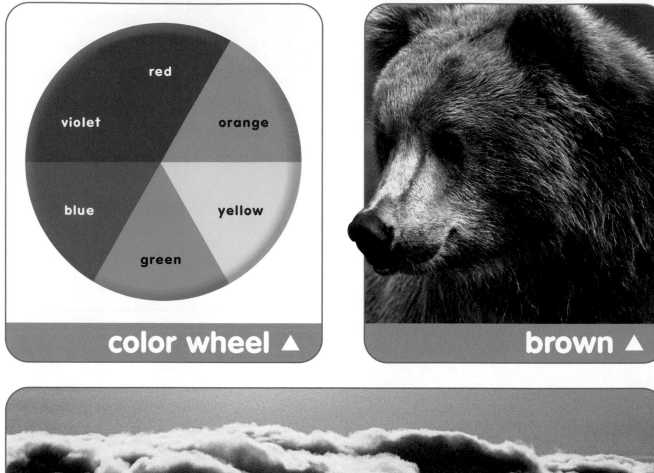

color wheel ▲

brown ▲

neutral colors ▲

value ▲

warm colors ▲

cool colors ▲

173

Texture

fluffy ▲

bumpy ▼

rough ▲

soft ▼

smooth ▲

scratchy ▼

174

Form

sphere ▼

cube ▼

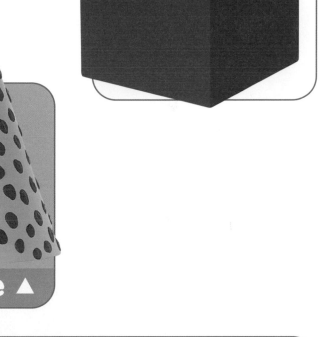

cone ▲

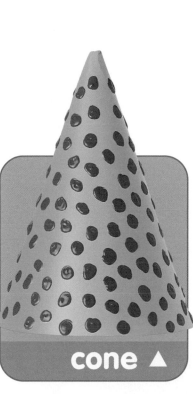

free form ▲

pyramid ▼

Space

positive space

negative space

horizon line

horizon line

background

foreground

Pattern

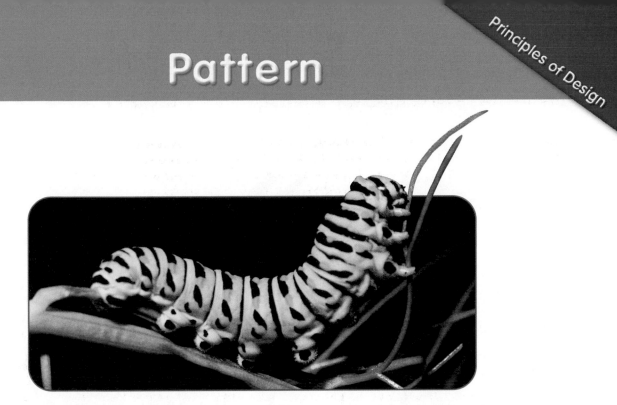

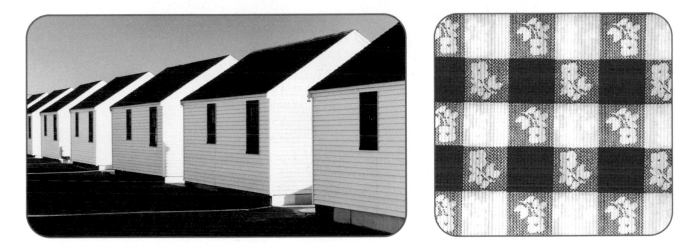

177

Rhythm and Movement

Balance

Emphasis

Variety and Unity

variety ▲

variety ▼

unity ▲

Gallery of Artists

Ansel Adams

(1902–1984) page 110

Sofonisba Anguissola

(1532–1625) pages 42–43

Thomas Hart Benton

(1889–1975) pages 62–63

Buckeye Blake

(1946–) page 91

Pieter Brueghel the Elder

(1525?–1569)

pages 102–103

Deborah Butterfield

(1949–) page 88

Eric Carle

(1929–) page 44

Mary Cassatt

(1844–1926) pages 130–131

Edna Crawford

(1968–) pages 56–57

Nancy Curry

(1961–) page 74

Edgar Degas

(1834–1917) page 114

Albrecht Dürer

(1471–1528) page 78

Abastenia St. Leger Eberle

(1878–1942) page 28

Flor Garduño

(1957–) page 111

Paul Gauguin

(1848–1903) page 104

Glenna Goodacre
(1939–) pages 82–83

Jonathan Green
(1955–) page 46

Ann Hanson
(1959–) page 78

Ichiryusai Hiroshige
(1797–1858) page 106

Katsushika Hokusai
(1760–1849) page 108

185

Gallery of Artists

Winslow Homer

(1836–1910) page 58

Luis Jaso

(1926–1983) page 38

Jasper Johns

(1930–) page 67

William H. Johnson

(1901–1970) page 132

Frida Kahlo

(1907–1954) pages 116–117

Phillip King

(1934–) page 86

Jacob Lawrence

(1917–2000) pages 76–77

Doris Lee

(1905–1983) page 33

Gerhard Marcks

(1889–1981) page 88

Henri Matisse

(1869–1954) pages 34, 106

Gerald McDermott

(1941–) pages 136–137

Claude Monet

(1840–1926) pages 49, 98

Grandma Moses

(1860–1961) pages 22–23

Miriam Tewaguna Nampeyo

(1956–) page 86

Georgia O'Keeffe

(1887–1986) pages 50–51

I. M. Pei
(1917–) page 95

Pablo Picasso
(1881–1973) pages 26, 36–37

Brian Pinkney
(1961–) page 24

Rembrandt van Rijn
(1606–1669) page 115

Diego Rivera
(1886–1957) pages 28, 48

Norman Rockwell
(1894–1978) page 124

Henri Rousseau
(1844–1910) pages 27, 72

Amos Supuni
(1970–) page 84

Wayne Thiebaud
(1920–) page 32

Suzanne Valadon
(1865–1938) page 52

Vincent van Gogh

(1853–1890) page 54

Frank Lloyd Wright

(1867–1959) pages 96–97

Jacob van Hulsdonck

(1582–1647) page 132

Stefano Vitale

(1958–) page 64

Glossary

abstract [ab′strakt]

Artwork with lines, shapes, and colors used in a way that does not look real. (page 36)

architect [är′kə•tekt]

A person who plans and designs buildings, bridges, or cities. (page 94)

architecture [är′kə•tek•chər]

The art and science of planning buildings. (page 94)

background [bak′ground]

The part of an artwork that seems farthest away. (page 98)

balance [bal′əns]

An arrangement of parts of an artwork that makes the parts seem equal. (page 112)

color wheel [kul'er (h)wēl]

A chart that shows primary and secondary colors in rainbow order. (page 47)

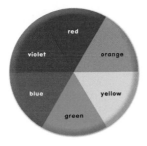

contrast [kon'trast]

A big difference between two parts of an artwork, like the difference between a light and a dark color. (page 114)

cool colors [kool kul'erz]

Colors such as blue, green, and violet that give a feeling of coolness and calmness. (page 48)

design [di•zīn']

A plan for the way lines, shapes, and colors are placed in an artwork. (page 118)

emphasis [em'fə•sis]

The use of size, shape, or color to make part of an artwork stand out. (page 106)

foreground [fôr′ground]

The part of an artwork that seems closest. (page 98)

form [fôrm]

An object that is not flat. It has height, width, and depth. (page 86)

free-form shapes

[frē′fôrm shāps]

Curved or uneven shapes that are not geometric. (page 34)

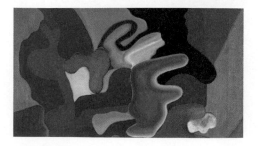

geometric shapes

[jē•ə•met′rik shāps]

Shapes used in math that have simple lines and curves, such as squares, triangles, and circles. (page 32)

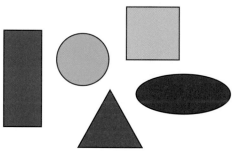

graphic art [graf′ik ärt]

Designs used on products, such as signs and TV ads. (page 138)

horizon line [hə•rī′zən līn]

The place where the land or water meets the sky. (page 58)

landscape [land′skāp]

An outdoor scene showing things like fields, trees, gardens, roads, and mountains. (page 98)

lines [līnz]

Marks that go from one point to another and that can be thin, thick, straight, curved, or zigzag. (page 26)

mood [mo͞od]

The way an artwork makes you feel, such as happy or sad. (page 54)

mosaic [mō•zā′ik]

An artwork made by fitting together small pieces of glass, tile, stone, or paper. (page 126)

movement [mo͞ov′mənt]
The feeling of motion, often made by using lines or patterns. (page 28)

O

organic shapes
[ôr•gan′ik shāps] Uneven or free-form shapes that look like things in nature, such as shapes of plants. (page 34)

outline [out′līn]
The line along the edge of a shape. (page 27)

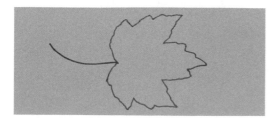

P

pattern [pat′ərn]
A design made by repeating lines, shapes, or colors. (page 66)

portrait [pôr′trit]
A picture of a person or a group of people. (page 38)

primary colors

[prī′mer•ē kul′erz]

The colors red, yellow, and blue. All other colors are made from these colors. (page 46)

print [print]

An artwork that is a copy, often made by pressing paint onto paper with an object or by using a stencil. (page 68)

relief sculpture

[ri•lēf′ skulp′chər]

A sculpture that has figures or objects that stand out from a flat background. (page 92)

repetition [rep•ə•tish′ən]

The use of lines, shapes, or colors over and over in a pattern. (page 67)

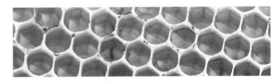

rhythm [ri<u>th</u>′əm]

A feeling of movement in an artwork, made by repeating lines, shapes, and colors. (page 72)

sculpture [skulp´chər]

An artwork, often made from stone, wood, metal, or clay, that has height, width, and depth. (page 88)

seascape [sē´skāp]

A picture that has a water setting, such as the ocean or the sea. (page 58)

secondary colors
[sek´ən•der•ē kul´erz]

The colors orange, green, and violet, each made by mixing two primary colors. (page 46)

self-portrait [self´•pôr´trit]

An artist's picture of himself or herself. (page 38)

shade [shād]

A darker color made by adding black to a color. (page 52)

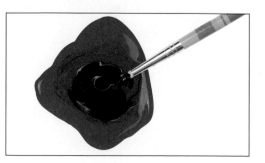

space [spās]

The empty areas within, between, above, below, or around objects or parts of an artwork. (page 88)

still life [stil līf]

An artwork that shows objects arranged in an interesting way. (page 132)

story cloth [stôr′ē klôth]

An artwork on cloth or other textiles that tells a story. (page 134)

subject [sub′jikt]

What an artwork is about. (page 108)

symbol [sim′bəl]

A person or object that has a special meaning and stands for something else. (page 128)

symmetry [sim′ə•trē]

The kind of balance created when both sides of something are the same. (page 112)

textiles [teks′tīlz]

Cloth or other fibers. (page 118)

texture [teks′chər]

The way a real object feels, such as bumpy or soft. (page 74)

tint [tint]

A lighter color made by mixing a color with white. (page 52)

unity [yoo′ni•tē]

The feeling that all the parts of an artwork belong together and that it is complete. (page 126)

value [val′yōō]

The lightness or darkness of a color. (page 52)

variety [və•rī′ə•tē]

The use of many different lines, shapes, or colors in an artwork. (page 132)

visual texture
[vizh′ōō•əl teks′chər]

The way something looks as if it would feel. (page 78)

warm colors
[wôrm kul′erz]

Colors such as red, yellow, and orange that give a feeling of warmth and energy. (page 48)

weaving [wēv′ing]

An artwork made by putting strips of paper, cloth, or other material over and under one another. (page 74)

Index of Artists and Artworks

Index

Index

Acknowledgments

For permission to reprint copyrighted material, grateful acknowledgment is made to the following sources:

Flint Public Library, 1026 East Kearsley, Flint, MI 48502-1994: "Two Little Friends" (Retitled: "Friends") from *Ring a Ring o' Roses: Finger Plays for Pre-School Children,* 11th Edition. Text copyright 1996 by Flint Public Library.

Tim Gallagher: From "Harvest Breeze" by Tim Gallagher in *Sunflower Road Journal.* Text copyright © 1990-2002 by Tim Gallagher.

Harcourt, Inc.: Cover illustration from *Coyote: A Trickster Tale from the American Southwest* by Gerald McDermott. Copyright © 1994 by Gerald McDermott.

HarperCollins Publishers: Cover illustration from *Dinosaur Bob and His Adventures with the Family Lazardo* by William Joyce. Copyright © 1988, 1995 by William Joyce. "Stardust Crooner" illustration from *The World of William Joyce Scrapbook* by William Joyce. Illustration copyright © 1997 by William Joyce.

Felice Holman: "At the Top of My Voice" from *At the Top of My Voice and Other Poems* by Felice Holman. Text copyright © 1970 by Felice Holman. Published by Charles Scribner's Sons.

Photo Credits

Page Placement Key: (t)-top (c)-center (b)-bottom (l)-left (r)-right

All photos property of Harcourt except for the following:

Frontmatter

6 (tr) Roger Wood/Corbis; 7 (tc) Miriam Tewaguna/Harcourt; (tr) Blackstar/Harcourt; 8 (tl) Araldo de Luca/Corbis; 12 Harper Collins Publishers; 14 (t) David Butow/Corbis Saba; 15 (t) Geoffrey Clements/Corbis; (b) LM Otero/AP/Wide World; 16 Francis G. Mayer/Corbis; 19 (tl) Royalty-Free/Corbis (cl) Alamy Images; 20 (bl) Alamy Images; (tr) Steve Terrill/Corbis; 21 Royalty-Free/Corbis; (c) Alamy Images; (b) Koji Kitagawa/Superstock.

Unit 1

22 Grandma Moses, Autumn/Collections of the Bennington Museum, Bennington, VT/Copyright 1985 Grandma Moses Properties Co., New York; 23 (b) Bettmann/Corbis; 24 Reprinted with the permission of Simon & Schuster Books for Young Readers, an imprint of Simon & Schuster Children's Publishing Division from Max Found Two Sticks by Brian Pinkney. Copyright © 1994 Brian Pinkney; 26 © 2006 The Estate of Pablo Picasso/Artist Rights Society (ARS), New York/Art Resource, NY; 27 (t) The Metropolitan Museum of Art, Gift of Marshall Field, 1939. (39.15); 28 (t) Schalkwijk/Art Resource, NY; 28 (b) Gift of Mrs. W.E. Chilton III/National Museum of Women in the Arts; 30 (tl) John and Lisa Merrill/Corbis; (bl) Owaki-Kulla/Corbis; 31 (tl) The Purcell Team/Corbis; (br) Andrew J.G. Bell; Eye Ubiquitous/Corbis; 32 Wayne Thiebaud, Desserts/The UBS Art Collection/Licensed by VAGA, New York; 33 (t) Gift of Wallace and Wilhelmina Holladay/National Museum of Women in the Arts; 34 © 2006 Succession H. Matisse, Paris/Artist Rights Society (ARS), New York/The Bridgeman Art Library; 36 © 2006 The Estate of Pablo Picasso/Artist Rights Society (ARS), New York/Digital Image © The Museum of Modern Art/Licensed by SCALA/Art Resource, NY; 37 (t) © 2006 The Estate of Pablo Picasso/Artist Rights Society (ARS), New York/Philadelphia Museum of Art/Corbis; (b) © 2006 The Estate of Pablo Picasso/Artist Rights Society (ARS), New York/Giraudon/Art Resource, NY; 38 (t) Antavio Morris/Parkview Elementary, Miami, FL; (b) Luis Jaso; 41 (b) Grandma Moses, Autumn/Collections of the Bennington Museum, Bennington, VT/Copyright 1985 Grandma Moses Properties Co., New York.

Unit 2

42 Ali Meyer/Corbis; 43 Scala/Art Resource, NY; 44 Eric Carle Studio; 46 Balloons For A Dime, 1996, Acrylic on Paper, 15" x 22"- Jonathan Green; 48 Diego Rivera Museum, Guanajuato, Mexico; 49 (t) Musee d'Orsay, Paris/Bridgeman Art Library, London/Superstock; 50 © 2006 The Georgia O'Keeffe Foundation/Artist Rights Society (ARS), New York/Columbus Museum of Art, Ohio, 51 (t) National Portrait Gallery, Smithsonian Institution/Art Resource, NY; (b) © 2006 The Georgia O'Keeffe Foundation/Artist Rights Society (ARS), New York/The Nelson-Atkins Museum of Art, Kansas City, Missouri (Gift of Mrs. Louis Sosland); 52 (l) Gustavo/ Constellation www.contellationart.org; (r) Private Collection/ Bridgeman Art Library; 54 The Metropolitan Museum of Art, Gift of George N. and Helen M. Richard, 1964. (64.165.2) Photograph copyright 1999/ The Metropolitan Museum of Art; 57 Edna Crawford; 58 Francis G. Mayer/Corbis; 60 (br) Francis G. Mayer/Corbis; 61 (b) Balloons For A Dime, 1996, Acrylic on Paper, 15" x 22"- Jonathan Green.

Unit 3

62 Lyle Peterzell/National Gallery of Art, Washington/Gift of the Artist/ Licensed by VAGA, New York, NY; 63 (b) Bettmann/Corbis; 64 Used by permission of HarperCollins Publishers; 66 The Newark Museum/Art Resource, NY; 67 (t) Whitney Museum of American Art, New York, USA/Bridgeman Art Library/Licensed by VAGA, New York, NY; 68 (b) Heather Burton/Shoreland Elementary; 70-71 (b) Erich Lessing/Art Resource, NY; 70 (l) Roger Wood/Corbis; 71 (t) Erich Lessing/Art Resource, NY; 72 (l) Norton Simon Collection, Pasadena, CA/Bridgeman Art Library; 72 (r) Jian Chen/Art Resource, NY; 74 Nancy Curry; 76 (t) Chris Eden/Eden Arts; (b) The Butler Institute of American Art/The Jacob and Gwendolyn Lawrence Foundation; 77 Hirshhorn Museum and Sculpture garden, Smithsonian Institution, gift of Joseph H. Hirshhorn, 1966/The Jacob and Gwendolyn Lawrence Foundation; 78 (l) On loan from Wallace and Wilhelmina Holladay/National Museum of Women in the Arts; 78 (r) Erich Lessing/Art Resource, NY; 81 (b) On loan from Wallace and Wilhelmina Holladay/National Museum of Women in the Arts.

Unit 4

82 Glenna Goodarce; 83 (b) Kelly-Mooney Photography/Corbis; 84 (l) Werner Forman Archive, Private Collection/Art Resource, NY; (r) Blackstar/Harcourt; 86 (l) Miriam Tewaguna/Harcourt; (r) Leeds Museums and Galleries (City Art Gallery), U.K./Bridgeman Art Library; 88 (l) Dave Bartruff/Corbis; (r) Deborah Butterfield/San Diego Museum of Art (Museum Purchase); 90 San Antonio Museum of Art, Nelson A. Rockefeller Mexican

Acknowledgments

Folk Art Collection; 91 (l) (r) National Cowboy & Western Heritage Museum; 92 (detail) Reunion des Musees Nationaux/Art Resource, NY; 94 Superstock; 95 (t) Dallas and John Heaton/Corbis; 96 Richard A. Cooke/Corbis; 97 (l) Angelo Hornak/Corbis; 97 (r) Underwood & Underwood/Corbis; 98 (t) Sotheby's, London/AKG, Berlin/SuperStock; 98 (b) Kacy/Ridgemont Elementary; 101 Dave Bartruff/Corbis.

Unit 5

102 Erich Lessing/Art Resource, NY; 103 (b) Historical Picture Archive/Corbis; 104 Collection of Mr. and Mrs. Paul Mellon/National Gallery of Art, Washington; 106 (l) © 2006 Succession H. Matisse, Paris/Artist Rights Society (ARS), New York/Pushkin Museum of Fine Arts, Moscow/SuperStock; (r) Ichiryusai Hiroshige/The Minneapolis Institute of Arts, Bequest of Richard P. Gale; 108 (t) The Metropolitan Museum of Art, H.O. Havemeyer Collection, Bequest of Mrs. H.O. Havemeyer, 1929 (jp1847) Photograph ©1991 The Metropolitan Museum of Art; 108 (b) Tori Rash/Hilltop Elementary, Lynnwood, WA; 110 (l) Roger Ressmeyer/Corbis; (r) Ansel Adams Publishing Rights Trust/Corbis; 111 (l) (r) Flor Garduno; 112 (l) Araldo de Luca/Corbis; (r) Giraudon/Art Resource, NY; 114 Reunion des Musees Nationaux/Art Resource, NY; 115 (t) Rijksmuseum, Amsterdam/SuperStock; 116 Banco de Mexico Trust/CNAC/MNAM/Dist Reunion des Musees Nationaux/Art Resource, NY; 112 (l) Araldo de Luca/Corbis; 117 (b) Photography Credit : Ben Blackwell/ San Francisco Museum of Modern Art; 118 (l) Danny Lehman/Corbis; (r) The Newark Museum/Art Resource, NY; 121 The Metropolitan Museum of Art, H.O. Havemeyer Collection, Bequest of Richard P. Gale.

Unit 6

122 Museum fur Volkerkunde, Wien oder MVK, Wien; 124 © 1966 The Rockwell Family Entities; 126 (t) Gilles Mermet/Art Resource, NY; (b) Kaela Mattson/St. John Central Middle School; 128 (bl) The British Museum; 129 (br) The British Museum; 130 The Detroit Institute of Arts 1978, gift of Edward Chandler Walker, accession number 08.8; 131 (t) The Metropolitan Museum of Art, Bequest of Edith H. Proskauer, 1975 (1975.319.1) photograph ©1998 The Metropolitan Museum of Art; (b) Armand Hammer Foundation, Los Angeles/Superstock; 132 (l) Smithsonian American Art Museum, Washington, DC/Art Resource, NY; 132 (r) Christie's Images/Superstock; 136 (l) Todd Bigelow/Black Star/Harcourt; 137 Gerald McDermott/Harcourt Trade; 138 (tl) (br) US Postal Service; 138 (tr) US Postal Service; 141 Armand Hammer Foundation, Los Angeles/Superstock.

Elements of Art

170 (tr) Getty Images; (br) Chase Swift/Corbis 174 (br) Royalty-Free/Corbis.

Gallery of Artists

Adams: AP/Wide World Photos; Anguissola: Scala/Art Resource, NY; Benton: Bettmann/Corbis; Brueghel: Historical Picture Archive/Corbis; Butterfield: Buck Butterfield, Inc.; Carle: Motoko Inoue/Eric Carle Studio: Cassatt: The Metropolitan Museum of Art, Bequest of Edith H. Proskauer 1975 (1975.319.1); Crawford: Harcourt/Edna Crawford; Curry: Nancy Curry; Degas: Giraudon/Art Resource, NY; Durer: Mary Evans Picture Library; Eberle: Kendall Young Library in Webster City, Iowa/Kendall Young Library; Garduno: Flor Garduno; Gauguin: AKG Images; Goodacre: Kelly-Mooney Photography/Corbis; Green: The History Makers; Hanson: Jason Hershman/Ann Hanson; Hiroshige: Peter Harholdt/Corbis; Hokusai: The Granger Collection; Homer: Bettmann/Corbis; Jaso: Arturo Jaso Y Asociados; Johns: Christopher Felver/Corbis; Johnson: Smithsonian American Art Museum, Washington, DC/The Art Resource, NY; Kahlo: Bettmann/Corbis; King: Phil Sayer/Royal Academy of Arts; Lawrence: Chris Eden/Eden Arts; Lee: National Museum of Women in the Arts; Marcks: AKG Images; Matisse: © 2006 Succession H. Matisse, Paris/Artist Rights Society (ARS), New York/AKG Images; McDermott: Gerald McDermott/Harcourt; Monet: Reunion des Musees Nationaux/Art Resource, NY; Moses: Bettmann/Corbis; Nampeyo: University of New Mexico Press; O'keeffe: National Portrait Gallery, Smithsonian Institution/Art Resource, NY; Pei: Phil Huber/Stock Photo; Picasso: © 2006 The Estate of Pablo Picasso/Artist Rights Society (ARS), New York/Philadelphia Museum of Art/Corbis; Pinkney: Hyperion Books for Children; Rijn: Scala/Art Resource, NY; Rivera: Bettmann/Corbis; Rockwell: Underwood & Underwood/Corbis; Rousseau: Erich Lessing/Art Resource, NY; Supuni: Deborah Tate-Collins of SABU, Inc./Sabu Inc.; Thiebaud: Christopher Felver/Corbis; Valadon: 2006 Artist Rights Society (ARS), New York/ADAGP, Paris/Christie's Images/SuperStock; Van Gogh: Reunion des Musees Nationaux/Art Resource, NY; Vitale: Stefano Vitale; Wright: Underwood & Underwood/Corbis.

Glossary

192 (bl) Rachel Epstein/PhotoEdit; 193 (tr) Lindsay Hebberd/Corbis; 194 (bl) Private Collection/Marilee Whitehouse-Holm/Superstock; 195 (tl) (cr) Alamy Images; (br) Index Stock Imagery, Inc. 196 (tl) Alamy Images; (tr) Roman Soumar/Corbis; 197 (tr) Alamy Images; (cr) Ralph A. Clevenger/Corbis; (br) George H. H. Huey/Corbis; 198 (tl) (bl) Alamy Images; 199 (bl) Michelle Garrett/ Corbis; (cl) Tretyakov Gallery, Moscow/AKG Berlin/SuperStock; 200 (tl) (br) Alamy images; (cl) Getty Images; 201 (cl) Douglas Peebles/Corbis; (bl) Bonhams, London/Bridgeman Art Library, London/SuperStock; (br) Photodisc Green/Getty Images.